Fall from Grace

Christopher Buckley

BkMk PRESS
THE UNIVERSITY OF MISSOURI–KANSAS CITY

Poetry by Christopher Buckley

Camino Cielo, 1997
A Short History of Light, 1994
Dark Matter, 1993
Blue Autumn, 1990
Blossoms & Bones, 1988
Dust Light, Leaves, 1986
Other Lives, 1985
Last Rites, 1980

BkMk Press of UMKC
University House
5100 Rockhill Road
Kansas City, MO 64110-2499

 Financial assistance for this book has been provided by the Missouri Arts Council, a state agency.

Library of Congress Cataloging-in-Publication Data

Buckley, Christopher, 1948-
    Fall from grace / Christopher Buckley.
        p.   cm.
    ISBN 1-886157-18-9
    I. Title.
    PS3552.U339F35   1998
    811'.54--dc21   98-22107
                                                            CIP

Cover art by Geanna Merola.
Cover design by Brad Kelley.
E-mail—   coolgrafix@gvi.net
Internet—   http://home.gvi.net/ ~ coolgrafix/

This book was typeset in Adobe Garamond, with titles set in BakerSignet.

Printed in the United States of America on acid-free paper.

10 9 8 7 6 5 4 3 2 1

The American Poetry Review/
Philly Edition   — Why I Am not yet a Zen Master

Black Warrior Review   — 4 Benches, 14 Orange Trees

Cimarron Review   — Ars Vita; The Poverty of Clouds

Crazyhorse   — Sleep Walk; Hymn to the Sky

Fish Stories   — Old Light

5 AM   — Morning, Dreaming of Empire

Hubbub   — The Knowledge of Oranges; Against the Blue

The Iowa Review   — Opera

The Kenyon Review   — Vacuum Genesis

New Letters   — Menorca, Spain: Poem about the Soul

POETRY   — Concerning Paradise

Quarterly West   — Astronomy Lesson; Death of the Poet, 1936;
                              Winter, No. 7 Miranda de Cala Corb; Lost Angel;
                              20 Years of Grant Application & State College Jobs

Solo   — Off Shore

Talking River Review   — Guardian Angel

Two Rivers Review   — Against Theory

Thanks to Sutton Hoo Press for a letter press, fine print chapbook of *Poem About The Soul*, and to Salmon Run Press for a chapbook of *The Poverty of Clouds*.

Special thanks to Jon Veinberg who first read and helped with this ms., and to Gary Young for his continued editing help. Thanks to Nadya Brown, Mark Jarman and Gary Soto for their responses and suggestions for these poems and for their support; and to Michelle Boisseau for final editing suggestions for the ms.

CONTENTS

Introduction

from a nominating letter for *Fall from Grace*.

Although Buckley has published eight previous collections of poetry, each one in my view is stronger than the preceding one, he has failed to receive the regard his work is due. For a poet who has been on the scene twenty years, publishing in the best journals, he is not nearly as well known as he should be.

From the first it was clear he had the gifts—a fine gift for the music of language, a sharp eye for physical detail, a large and rich vocabulary, and a deep concern for the earth and all of us who inhabit it. I believe this new collection shows him at his best, reaching out for an inclusive poem that emotionally embraces as much of our worldly estate as poetry can contain. Pay special attention to such poems as "Against The Blue," "Astronomy Lesson," and "The Poverty of Clouds," and you will hear a singular poetic voice in our poetry, one of the most lyrical and genuine of any poet his age.

I have been following his work since he published *Last Rites* in 1980 and have noted the steady growth reflect itself in a confidence of craft and a willingness to encounter the most thorny and puzzling human dilemmas with ever increasing wisdom and good spirits: this is the work of an experienced and deeply moral individual willing to face the facts of this century with a steady eye and an open heart, this is poetry that should be known by a large American public; for if taken to heart, it can help us survive with dignity.

Philip Levine

FALL FROM GRACE

Once, in the white sky there was
a beginning, and I happened to notice
and almost glimpsed what to do.
But now I have come far
to here, and it is away back there.
Some days, I think about it.

from "In The White Sky"
William Stafford

I

The Poverty of Clouds

Anything is enough if you know how poor you are.
— Larry Levis

We want things. Right now,
because whatever we have
on earth—this railing for example
around a small balcony four flights up—
never holds back the sky's impoverished weight,
or the predictable transaction of morning
offering neither mystery or revelation . . . .

But I'm at that age where I'll just settle
for my breath, the clear enclave
of memory at this blue hour
where there are only two restaurant workers
waiting at the bus stop, in the cold,
their white kitchen smocks flapping
in the wind. And they look really,
nothing at all like angels,
each holding his grocery bag
with old Adidas sneakers—
work shoes bruised with grease—
speaking a Spanish
I always half understand.

The railing bleeds rust through
the tacky surface of the paint,
and my thumb prints add up
like the first dull clouds floating by
against the flat backdrop of air—
the only reliable company
desire ever keeps.

*

I'm gone now long enough from home
that no matter how much I want
to walk down State Street to Cañon Perdido,
turn right for the California Theater,
go up to the kid left waiting for his ride
and pat him on the shoulder, I should know
that he hasn't stood there for thirty years,
that soon it will be dark
and the same low sky over the mesa
will send up a smattering of clouds
like feathers from a pigeon
just struck by a car.

And it shouldn't matter anymore
what happened to my one pair
of Florsheim wing tips, the ones I saved
all summer for so I'd have what passed
for style that last year in school
when we were all wearing white socks,
those polished cordovans gleaming ridiculously
beyond my means. I must have worn them
to death, or to dust, or left them behind
when I went off to college, and one day
some poor soul at the Salvation Army
spotted them and shined the toes
with the greasy sleeve of his raincoat
before he shuffled off deliriously
despite the uneven heels,
the ground down soles.

*

When didn't we want something
from the world every day
regardless of the fact that some sky
off in the future was filling
with loss, waiting to resemble itself

as vaguely as a cloud?
This would be fate, out of the past,
a little fog burning off the coast,
a lesion on your calf invisibly
growing there since you were seven—
the damage, the Dr. says, all done
before you're 20—Time just keeping
everything from happening at once.

But there was something
glowing in me back there—
not 100 watts of wisdom, for I sat
in the back of class, day-dreaming
out the window, watching for the clouds
that would spell rain and let us out early.
Nor was it a brief glimmer
of grace falling on my hands
through the high windows of the church
that lit the quick fuses in my veins
and shot me out of there for what
blood alone was worth.
Wisdom would not have helped
my dog-eager heart which loved
the slow down-sifting of days
and what few illuminated moments
the angels in their grey uniforms doled out—
the extra recess after mass, glazed
donuts and hot chocolate, the sugar rush
that had us leaping from trees and off
lunch tables yelling, Jesus, Holy Smokes!
I went around looking up and expecting
the next wonderful thing to appear.
So if anyone remembers air—the invisible
celebrity of breath—it's me; it was pure
as high as the clouds then went—
my arms full of the mystic
sources of dust and a bit of wind going red
over the dark shoulders of the oaks.

Above the peaks of the Santa Ynez
the late clouds were ivory and belled as yucca blooms—
that calligraphy, oh, I could read it clearly then,
could diagram every inference
in my grey uniform shirt as I raced out of class
with a hand colored map of yellow, green, and blue
on which I'd inscribed Addis Ababa, Constantinople,
and Timbuktu. I climbed the acacia saying
those names among the confabulating birds,
commanding for a moment all that space
and time waving from my hand,
aided and abetted by the sky.

Where else was I going?
Everything rushing by,
leaving only a small hesitancy
on the air, the way the Southern Pacific "Daylight"
swooshed past at 4:15 each day
and was gone straight south
toward the copper sun which gleamed
like the penny I'd placed on the tracks
and never found . . . . I stood there
until I could see nothing but a vacant haze,
until the rails—so polished by the grinding insistence
of steel—mirrored the sky and quit singing.

*

Because he did not want to be loved
for his money, Wittgenstein gave away
his inheritance and moved to Switzerland
to teach at an elementary school.
He walked out beneath the Alps, the clouds,
their blank circumstance and shadow
that had him whistling difficult passages
of Mahler from memory, thinking about suicide.

Each night he went to the movies and sat
in the first row where all the images would blur,
and from there, his brooding theories
about the indigence of language
rained down.
                    I was as afraid of rain
as any other earthly thing, and in those days
my father employed phrases to comfort me
and disguise the day—just a little haze, or drizzle,
mist, heavy fog, light sprinkles. Either way,
it was there where I pined for a horizon line
blue as a lizard's belly—a grey
against the only realms of breath I knew.

                          *

Back at that sky, clear and colorless,
the first of autumn, wild ivy lined white
at the edges—let's just sit here and see
if the camphor leaves will speak,
if the rain clouds will intercede
with their old cavalcade of admonitions,
if we will ever escape that longing
for happiness, that landscape of old light
everlasting in our blood.

By the bear-shaped lake of Oso Flaco
stars rose yellow as the coreopsis,
I collected whale bone, seal spine and sand dollars
that turned quickly back to sand.
In Ensenada, children reach out, begging
as if their arms were broken,
their cotton shirts dirty as the dim sky
as they arrive on every corner
with the certainty of clouds—
                              their skin
dark as the air beneath every shade tree

in Roeding park, where no one now,
I think, sits on that picnic table
beneath the starving redwood,
opening a box of Marlboros, lighting one
after another with controlled resignation,
exhaling perfectly detached rings
that dissolve into nothing,
into blue halos that hold a second
as if there were something celestial
in the first punished light of dawn,
a cloud of smoke, or ordinary despair.

I only have to return here once
in a great while to keep up my notes
on the composition of grief,
the insolvency of even the most
casual desire. The usual green paint
builds up over who once loved whom
carved into the wood—initials,
dates, a star drifting off the edge,
and overhead, stars falling like small change
through the hands of the dark . . . .

I can only underestimate
the physics, the failure of particles
which account for us, and for loss.
But not in any measurable sense
for that handful of Ones
left on the counter where he's not
drinking alone, and peacefully,
not for that plank on the park table
where no one sits flicking a cigarette
with its comet trail of sparks
toward the trash can, or Blackstone Ave.
where he'll at last head out for home,
all the windows of the old Plymouth down
to feel alive again, to feel that rich

blood freight of summer,
the honeysuckle and hay weighing
the dew-cooled air on 41,
where there is only the fading moon,
its burden of ash and borrowed light
as he feels the world blowing right through him,
as if he wasn't there . . . .

Hymn to the Sky

Romero Canyon, Santa Barbara

I didn't have visions of angels then
mending the miraculous hem of dusk,
golden and unthreaded across the west,
nor take into my boy's arms anything
but the unpalpable body of doubt
about my abbreviated stay in the world
as my prayers ascended the silk trees
and flames crested each leaf. I couldn't see
that the avowed subject of those trees
was air—a bright blue breathing out
without a trace of us on earth.

I only climbed the prosaic oaks thinking
I could hold my place, figure out the remainder
of a grand design, which leaves would go
to pieces in my hands, which in the rising winds
of dawn. Light was the thing, the set theory
and sum inside my veins and eucalyptus
boughs—I had a ransom of romantic verse,
I had some clouds, and not one theorem
to solve the unequal equation of desire
with night spiking up its black staves
all along those burning hills.

*

I was a guest in a house of white clouds
as the days reset their small tables of light.
The sunrise haze above the olive trees was all—
dew on the bay laurel rising,
carried over into the sallow collar-band of dusk,
into each litany of thistle and onion grass
green as the first idea of rain.

12

Bird that brings the past back in broken notes,
cantata slipping over the sandstone ridge
where all my old stars have gone, dust
still glimmers there, faithless
as the wine palms of Eden. I know enough now
to listen for music as faint as breathing
circling the wristbone of the blue.

*

So lately, I've been leaning toward the sky,
and the Dark Matter humming invisibly there,
the un-shining stuff of the universe
is just another dust we haven't named
like one more angel fallen from grace.
I should help him collect his star-colored blood
from the spikes of ice plant, This one I've seen
on the shoreline in his baseball cap and beard,
with clipboard and pen, parsing the spindrift,
refuting the sea that knows us as nothing
more than phosphorus and a little ash.

I don't want to worry any longer
about a little smoke lifting over the bay
or the grey thumbprint on the horizon
we will soon enough become. Let the years
walk off in their saffron robes, I will gloss
the language of the trees, hell-bent on
here and now, the handful of stars flung
like an infinite trail of crumbs above
the sleeping hills where crows submit
their dark estimates pine to pine—
all the rest getting to me in time.

*

Here I sit in my bleached blue shirt,
flag of my only country, turning back
to each thing I might have been—the water's
anapest over rocks, the thin light lingering
where the waxwings were—before I am reduced
by the ordinary progressions and discords of time
to our numbered and essential salts.

Always, half a moon rising over the road
of the past. Where have I been all my life?
Isn't there a bird missing in that field?
Beneath the old sycamore, I take a little wine,
and shining so, remember the orange groves,
their green verses across the hills, from where
I've always held the clouds in high regard.

The Knowledge of Oranges

One Saturday, only 9 or 10 and on my own, I took off
on my red and man-sized Schwinn across the foothill roads
to run the big hill to the bottom for speed alone
and round about head out to that small grove where
a house or two pushed the boulders and big oaks back.
Standing on the pedals side to side, I soon shifted
flying into 3rd, and streamlined and leaning low, picked up
so much speed that hand brakes were not near enough,
and so screeching, sailed straight through the STOP
into the intersection where the one car descending
that mountain road all morning had me squarely in its sights—
a ton and a half of Ford Country Squire thundering down
and blinding in its chrome. There was an instant—
a frame where fast time froze while she hit her brakes—
where I, in slowest motion, went swooshing barely
by the grille.
           Our gazes locked, my face flashing
red with terror; hers with shock and then exasperation
as I flew by not a feather's width to spare, and she shot on,
everything only my fault had I been a bloody smear
for most of a mile, or mangled among the blooming trees.
I stopped in the roadside weeds, arms reaching up over my head
to the handle bars as if arrested by the sky, right leg
caught over the high cross bar as I tried to get my breath.
Then a minute or more before I climbed off and pulled
the foxtails from the chain and walked my bike up hill
to the next road, level to the right.
                What can you know
at 9 or 10 no matter what? Not much cuts through clearly
and marks you for the light, strips the gauze and glitter
from your eyes. But I'd been jolted in my day dreaming days
and knew I'd come, for nothing, within inches of the dark—
that boarding house of death I'd hardly thought about at all.
All that in the rush and blood-buzz in my bones

to say I'd been spared for no reason I could then or ever
know on earth. And though it was a certain warning
to pay attention to the world, I shook my head, coasted
along a while and soon pedaled toward the white fragrance
of the grove to grab a low-hanging orange or two, drop them
in the saddlebag beneath the seat and beat it to my hideout
atop an outcrop where I took a still minute to hold my palms
up and count my ten fingers out. Then I held both oranges
up against the blue—emblem of my life given to me twice,
easy grace for such sleepy souls as I. Peeling one, the spray
of acid stung my eyes and the warm juice stained my thumbs
as I sensed the sun's slow fire pumping through my veins,
as I relished the sweetness I held so lightly in my hands.

Sleep Walk

Fourteen and I knew from nothing—
but there I was in the darkened gym
to get some idea. Someone was stacking the 45's
and my friend Carlson was doing The Stroll
with Maryann Garland, gliding around the corners
of the basketball court with that strut, scuff, and easy slide.
I knew Surf Music and Motown cold, but even if
I worked up nerve to ask a girl to dance, there was no way
when it came to the Stomp, the Mash Potato,
those spins, dips, and twists kids were pulling off
like varieties of religious experience.

As recently as 8th grade, in classes the nuns
roped us into after school, I had only managed
a reluctant fox trot, as if I were dragging my shoes
through a dance floor of fudge. And those meager skills
had only lead to heartbreak and Virginia Cortez,
the dark stars of her eyes burning through me
at a party where parents drank coffee in the kitchen
and came out every quarter hour to keep lights on
in the living room. She leaned her head into my shoulder
and shorted out the entire network of circuits
in my skin—and though we barely moved across
the carpet to the Statues and "Blue Velvet," sparks
stung our hands and pulled us into a world where
you could get lost in no time . . . .
                            So there I was, fourteen
and through with love, putting on my best Bob Mitchum
tough-guy face, saying I'd seen it all already, and so what?
But someone switched the disks to Doo Wop, the Flamingos
and slow oldies, and the whole floor of dancers froze,
swaying only a fraction to "In The Still of The Night"
before Santo & Johnny's "Sleep Walk"
ground any pretense of movement to a halt

with its bone-deep bass laying down a line of hormones
like an infection in the blood—the high, sliding lead
seeming to lift all the sighing dreamers
out the transoms of the gym into the starlight spinning
through the blue spring night.
                                    I'd been watching a couple
in the middle—the girl, a pageboy blond, all curves
in a cotton dress, and a tall guy from the team—seniors
who'd been melting into each other all evening,
enough steam rising there to press a dozen shirts.
Both her arms hung on his neck, his arms wound around
her waist—as hot as it then got before you were thrown out
and called into the office during home room on Monday.
What wouldn't I give to be them in that dim light
and crepe paper, all confidence and careless in love?

But I knew from nothing—no one told me to be careful
what you wish for . . . . And two and a half years turned me
loose in that exact spot, arms around Kathy Quigley,
eyes closed, feet stuck to the gym floor and "Sleep Walk"
stringing out a last legitimate embrace. It was time to walk out
those double metal doors, rubbing our eyes, dizzy
with our own tranced blood buzzing in the dark.
We had to kiss quickly so she could get home by 12:00—
the world still that careful and slow.
                                    I'd drive around
for an hour, up and down State, pull into Petersons for a shake,
circle the town, radio off, cruising with the windows down,
with that twang and ground swell bass from Santo & Johnny
still pulsing in my head, sure this was everything there was
despite college coming, and the war. I looked up into the night
where the stars slurred like the notes in that song
and wished again, as if I knew what I wanted . . . .

II

Opera

Upgraded from economy class, I'm flying down the freeway
feeling rich as God, behind the wheel of a silver, full-size
sedan—quad stereo, cruise control, gold glowing digital clock—
and for a minute I think of that article on the Sultan of Brunei
checking out from a hotel and leaving enough money in tips
to fund disease research for a year. But soon I'm satisfied
just floating through a corridor of pines, popping in my tape
of Carerras, Domingo, and Pavarotti. A chorus of blue above me,
a few arpeggios of clouds to the right, not unlike the sky
over the Baths of Caracalla where they're singing—three ancient
stories of brick still standing on the edge of Rome. We came
across it one summer as workers were erecting the stage
and high dusty towers for *Aida*—40 then, and just beginning
to listen . . . .
        70 mph and I'm transported by the wind-
swell of the orchestra, lifted by the violins, brought back
to earth by violoncellos, the heart still climbing that white
ladder of hope with "Rondine al Nido," Pavarotti's power
surge spiking current along my arms. I let the tape rewind—
this is serious, I keep hearing, we are all going to die,
hopelessly though, and at last in love with the world.
By now, most my aspirations let go, blown by me like litter
along the road, I'm just happy to be breathing, to be soaring
in such company, to have a heart thumping its own sprung notes.

No one is going to sleep until Pavarotti has an answer
to the riddle and claims the starry heart of Turandot—
now all three encore "Nessun Dorma," and in the bridge
all the angels sing, sodality in the last movement of lost air.
I too want to fly, to know the ineluctable extravagance
of the spirit about to slip out of the tux, beyond the fingertips
into the night sky.
        But I have to rent a car to hear
these tapes punched up to the proper brick-shaking valence.

I have to leave town, get away from young friends at parties
where the angels all wear red shoes, where I'm told Dwight Yoakam
is "Bakersfield Opera," where CDs are stacked like potato chips—
either trash bands like Pilonidal Cyst, Meat Puppets, and
Mud Honey, or time fractures from the 70s, Hendrix, Led Zeppelin,
and the Chambers Brothers. Nothing close to carrying off the sky
like Verdi or Puccini—in heaven, they have to be cooking Italian!

Friends my age are all listening to opera—Pavarotti's Richter Scale
and range proving there's another level, and though the register,
like the body, is giving way to gravity, there is something
there just above us.
         The astral body must be like this,
all sentience and incorporeal as sound. I want some singing
about that—all the red and blue bright threads spun out
from our hearts, spooled above the gilt-edged clouds,
above the scraps of flesh and diminuendos of ordinary time.
I want this feeling of atoms falling out of the crystal orbits
of the earth, yet reclaimed by arias, by cavatinas.
Carrerras recovering from cancer, Domingo's good looks
going south, Pavarotti barely able to move—yet each lifting
past the burning limits of the dark. And conducting everything,
Zubin Mehta—surely that has to be an angel's name?
But this is serious, we are all going to die.

for Bill Matthews

Off Shore

for Mark Jarman

Fifteen and what was there to do? The world so flat and slow,
Arthur Godfrey and Andre Kostelanetz still somewhere
on the radio? So I'd charge out on my Honda trail bike
to the beach and check the swell, the disposition of the tide,
see if the breeze was blowing off shore, holding
the wide waves up.
                              From under a friend's beach-front porch,
I'd haul out my dinged-up board and wax it down,
scratch through the soup to waves lined up and pealing
perfectly left to right at Shark's, Miramar, or Fernald Point.

Holy Days of Obligation—public school kids sweating it out
till 3:00—we had the best breaks to ourselves. And sometimes,
like palpable grace, the translucent sets steamed through
shoulder-high and sprayed spindrift back against the sky
as I took the drop and trimmed it up, nose-riding to shoot the curl,
then back pedaling as if walking on coals to kick out
before the shore break and the crunch.
                                        Was there nothing
clear but that compulsion to climb out of myself onto the air
into that surging life and green whorl we cut through
but would not think beyond, numb and knee paddling
for the next outside set, the overhead walls tunneling
into the world and wholly apart from it?
                                        What light
this now throws on every other thing is almost lost—
like me then, it was only what it was, burning wholly
at any cost on its own elemental terms. To step out
beyond the scene leaves me in my stiff, un-soaring bones
and short of breath, when what I want is the cheap grace
of a body that breaks through space smoothly as the sun,
my mind clear as water, with its unconscious message quick
to my heart and lungs to breathe.

                              Even in February,
my legs gone grey as ice, I caught the rip-tide out
and slotted in, cranked a bottom turn and, grabbing a rail,
ripped through the tumbling trough to hang five pearling
forward off the board, careless and coming up easily
as a cork for the only reason that I was, and knew it there—
the salt and sea water chorusing in my blood and every
singing molecule of my skin.
                              Back up the hills at dusk,
the roads were empty, and there was next to nowhere
then to go. There was a Hi-Fi and my stack of 45's;
there were hundreds of dollars and a year or more
between me and a car.
                              Each morning, fog burning
off the oaks and pines, and I'd kick-start my bike
with some Stratocaster surf tracks still pumping
like quick sets of waves over a reef in my mind,
and make the early run to find the break,
the glassy tubes—my life calmly racing out
in front of me, wind clearing the frothy light—
most everything still before me there in 1963, and
everywhere in the world I had to be was there.

Vacuum Genesis

If you don't know how you got somewhere
you don't know where you are
          — James Burke

"A blue-million of 'em" my aunt always says—we were looking up
above Kentucky for a meteor shower and saw only an unmitigated
skyline; too much light too close to us, all those electrons going
to town, diffuse between the air around us. I'd seen it once before,

the night full of flares, sparking out of nowhere, vanishing again
into the otherwise empty scope of things. But a vacuum, it turns out,
is never truly empty. Even when the universe was nothing more
than a held breath, a vast lake flat with helium and hydrogen,

it only took a hiccup in that slick molecular mix for every ten billion
quark/anti-quark pairs created and annihilated in that first blast
toward light, to leave one extra quark behind—a tiny surplus—all
that was required to evolve the chain link clusters and whirligigs

we point to today. Apparently something can emerge from nothing—
virtual particles buzz like halos around real ones, and that pretty much
accounts for biological creatures like ourselves who look up and petition
the pinpoint night, who find at our fingertips language for that dimension-

less place, name animals and plants, the spins on sub-atomic particles,
their "flavors"—*Strange* and *Charmed*. Untied from the unities and set
stumbling about, we arrived at parallel universes—on the bubble, stacked up,
bottled, bright ships on a black expanding shelf, not a supporting speck

of evidence for something that may or may not be there, wherever
"there" might be. We had a ranch house on the coast, a yard burning
with wild nasturtiums, clusters of blue pines and periwinkle,
and a station wagon on time which let us slip unnoticed through

the streets of suburbia, no one imagining mother and I sharing
a can of tomato soup with fried bologna on wheat all those nights
father was working late. We sat in the kitchen, the GE radio—
purple, plastic, the size of a bread box—on the table. Its one clock-like

dial coaxed in music always less interesting than the warped tones
and oscillations I found flipping between stations. I pulled in the blank
imponderable sounds of space and peeked through the hundred holes
in the Masonite backing to the tubes—orange filaments glowing

beneath their dust-dark caps like the tails of comets—and each night
hadn't the least idea where it all was headed. Soon enough, TVs appeared,
and by the end of the 50s the future was clear in a set whose mahogany
cabinet doors opened to Buck Rogers, Rocky and The Space Pirates,

or Saturday mornings of posses and bandidos, six-shooters firing
all over Malibu or Chatsworth, the tree-thick back lots of L.A., glorious
in black & white where heroes galloped off over the sunset hills and
disappeared in a cloud of dust. After staring at a bombardment of electrons

all morning, I was sent out to play in our wide neighborhood, the boundaries
of which I knew well. I was tethered to the daylight's long string unraveling
from all that vacant and unquestioned space beyond our drive, and charged
only to find my way home before the first star appeared again in the sky.

Guardian Angel

...he may be that blue issuing from a tailpipe
of a car idling in the road.
                              —Gary Soto

Out late, racing around in my father's MG, four wheels drifting
through the hairpin turn, snaking the S curves by the Bird Refuge,
I was lame-brained and lost it, came up sideways on a cement wall,
one with my name—*boboso, shit head, Joe Mama*—sprayed all over it.
For a second I grew calm, almost resigned to my fate,
then the sprung torque of two revolutions bit, spun back, and flung me
singing *Jesus Crippled Christ!* across two oncoming lanes
toward that mud and shallow drink where, stomping on the brakes,
I stopped short with nothing more than the black boulevard of night
whizzing past my ears.

                   Lucky—in a way—no traffic or I'd have been
grease, a glossy smear for a quarter mile. But it had to be more than luck
that lifted me through the blind intersection at Indio Muerto and Voluntario
where Orsua, Desmond Olivera and I were T-boned by a cancer-infested
late 40s Merc doing fifty if it was doing five. Airborne, kitty-corner,
we mowed down an oleander hedge and nailed a pepper tree before spinning
out in someone's front yard. Out of nowhere, two guys in black bowling shirts
looked in the window and said, "Futas! you crazy kids give us the booze now
before the cops get here."

                   We counted our ten fingers, looked in the mirror
for our teeth. Who was watching then, who knew we were coming
and had been standing unnoticed in the street lamp's violet arc, slowly
cleaning his fingernails of the past so there would be room for us to arrive
unscathed and dazed? Who put his hands over my eyes at impact as I lost count
of those dark seconds forever until I came to rest cattywampus on that lawn?
How else to explain—sober as scientists and climbing out the driver's side
without a scratch, all the parts in our Brylcreemed hair still in place?

                         How else
could I have edged away from the dark licks of Death as he rode next to me
each day I drove the foothills home—peeling a tangerine with his teeth,

his grey skin all but invisible as he squeaked across the vinyl seat, rolling
the wind wing out to spit and call up little swindles of dust where my '59 Chevy
fish-tailed on retreads slick as seals and its wide fins carved their initials
in a sycamore before sending me and the whole two-toned caboose headlong
toward an arroyo? Who was on the shoulder with his thumb out, whistling
an old Perry Como tune as my axle snagged an oak sapling and yanked me
to a stop—hubcaps flying off like lost galaxies, front tires spinning just over
the edge of night?

        Again, I walked away, but I didn't hear bodiless voices
sing above me in a code known only to the dozing clouds and distant spheres.
And though I paused staring up into the oil-blue vault, I knew I wouldn't see
some chariot charge across the sky in an alphabet of flame or revelation,
or even warning for the unconscious conduct and weak vessel of my blood.
Wasn't I 17 and already living in paradise on the California coast,
most all the documents of pain yet to be delivered or misfiled in a place
as forlorn as Philadelphia? Wasn't this just the motoring life
that had you slathering Bondo onto your lead-sled with numb enchantment,
and, which at worst, left you wondering, whistling when you looked back?
Yet I heard something snap, like a green branch where no one was,
or if not that, a sound like tumblers clicking in a lock, a tiny brass weight
plopped on the metal plate of a scale . . . .

        All this came rushing back
as I was about to cross the swirl of headlights laser-beamed around Logan Circle—
a humming hoop of light with cars switching lanes like electrons,
where the civic fountain was fumbling a few coins of froth and I never
should have been directing my attention the very moment a black sedan
shot right by my shoes, a spot where I'd just jumped back, startled
the instant before by honking and a bonfire of brake lights ascending
the dull air not twenty yards away:

        some bum—not my father—
but with the same galvanized hair fanned swan-like, TV evangelist–style,
was almost clipped by an Infinity J-30, and despite curses and a chorus
of horns, was holding his ground with a low, bending sweep of his arm,
a less than sober version of a matador's best move. Then, running
his hand through his hair like a symphony conductor, he threw his head
back, looking skyward past the trees frozen there like cracks in the dome
of dusk, and proceeded across the stream of lights as a gust caught
the tails of his greasy raincoat, and set them flapping like wings.

28

Lost Angel

¿Ahora qué hago con éste y con el otro?
—Neruda, "To Envy"

Above this valley basin, I'm examining a cloud or two for clues,
for any flesh-grey scrap left by the one separated shoulder blade
by blade from me as I stepped out of that filtered realm
onto the sidewalks in sensible brown shoes, in line for advancement
to the scholarly legions of the halt and lame and a final ascendancy
to the congress of the heavily bored and boring, and thus
ever after found myself lost when compared to his inventions
and reclassification of the air.
                           God knows what I was trying
to get through as fast as I possibly could. He probably sauntered off
into the hills, sunstruck as oat straw or thistle stalks, singing something
that was part wind, part mountain creek. Maybe he climbed on a boxcar,
invisible for the most part against the white lettering on the door,
and found work in the strawberry fields of Oxnard
or as a night clerk in a rooming house in downtown Camarillo—
I gave it little thought. I knew what was good for me
and caught the bus on time, moved east.
                                Now everything
that the sky back there said I dispute. That sky has erased and rewritten
its clouds until I see a childhood sitting on its stool, counting dim fingers
against the shadowed wall—there are ten or twenty, and mother reading
from the Golden Book the cautious tale about a fisherman, wishes,
a talking fish—the fire enunciating its syllables of flame, the house otherwise
dark and lost beyond the trees . . . .
                            But forty years down the road
my heart is doing double-takes—the bus driver with my retreating hair,
thin crown of sunlight reflecting off his head. And he looks up shining
with grease in the car repair—my beard above my denim shirt, a little wound
of ink or motor oil leaking from his left breast pocket. I'm worrying
for him, a silver pool of anti-freeze at his feet, which, in one world
or another, might indicate an accident, or fall from grace.

But he just passes a rag the color of old fire over the brake drum until
it takes on a beatific gleam, then taps some embers from his pipe
against his palm and goes back about the business of the earth's broken
vehicles, humming "My Blue Heaven." I recognize the Flying Dutchman
tobacco on the air and remember tossing my pipes out fifteen years ago
to avoid another dark fate. I look out to the passing band of cloud,
back to the repair bay where he's getting on contentedly with the nuts
and bolts of his life—a life, given my dismal performance in science
and in math, which could just as easily have been mine. We're equally light
in the wallet, but one of us knows the scale and dynamics of the wind
and the other his intractable part in gravity.

What else should I be thinking
of at this late date—the electricity of the universe delivering itself
in waves or subtle packets through every equally unknowing thing
to the tips of my fingers, and the blank blue hum around my skin
extending itself like breath, exhaling slowly, a second part of some essential
shining?

Of course.

But as often as not I find myself brooding
among back streets and alleys where I once lived happily enough,
where I now feel snakebit, the dingy bones of the spirit showing through
as I stare into the second-hand bookstore or The Chicken Pie Shop for faces
I might dimly know. Until I'm taking a breather, leaning against an ash,
an elm, looking into a back yard as he comes out the screen door
with my shoulders, my fur-brown sweater slouching past the back pockets.
Only he's lost some weight thanks to an ambitionless heart; and sure,
I get it now, he never left Fresno—dead center of the state with its flat
linen light and freight yards, its seraphic miles of almonds and plum,
crepe myrtle and fig, Basque Hotels and seven course sheep-herder meals.
He never wised up and took off in search of career enhancement,
half a step up the ladder of merit at a time, the ladder of sand.
Hell, he's still living at the bottom of Arthur Street, the iffy end
of the Tower District with its greasy cafes, appliance shops and one sad
music store with its picture window from which no piano has ever sold.
He's a hundred yards from the tracks, just across from the pitiful zoo
where each sundown peacocks call over the redwoods like abandoned souls.
It's the same slat board house on blocks, the yellow faded to a bit of fog,

old steam rising against more steam.

He bends one knee, confiding
to the irises, their white and topaz wings—he tends the chilies,
slicing one in half and testing it on his tongue for the burning coal it is.
The TV antenna still spreads its bones against the sky, pulling in
its three blurry channels. That old log of a Rambler is parked out front,
the one metal ash can without its lid in back—fruiting mulberry
to the right, three slender nectarines along the left, the jays eating
everything under the sun. How the high industry of the world seems
to have passed this place by.

But he's unbothered as the birds,
as he re-stakes poles for the last tomatoes and runner beans,
dead-heads the brick-colored roses, three a side, along the hard pan walk.
I can see his other shoes on the porch, those old golden Nikes
with the nubby tread and slim blue wings along each side.
About 5:00 he'll slip them on and fly straight up past Palm
then back down to Olive and the deli. He's still getting away
with that mortadella and provolone, bottles of thick Italian red—
he's not worrying himself to death about his health. And there's the burlap
onion bag, so he must still go up the tracks collecting splinters of creosote
for the fire place, almost floating in the dust there beneath the pink
oleanders, profuse in the evening sun.

He's practical, and takes easily
to his tasks—he's tearing a few yellowed pages out of an old Latin text
to start a small yard fire for the brown tomato leaves and grocery sack
of weeds. He's pushing up the sleeves of that sorry sweater, standing there
in his white-as-paper skin, almost disappearing in the first plumes of smoke,
then reappearing at a picnic table with a water glass of that wine,
waving a long finger toward the fire like a conductor.
And he can just about sing—Pavarotti on the portable tape player
with "Panis Angelicus" and he goes along for the first few bars, a few
starlings on the wires help him out, and so he is not without friends,
complexity, or art—or sense, as he switches over to whistling as
the melody rises above his range.

The song over, he gets up and
pulls the rusted Lawn Boy from the shed—high harmonies of wrenches,
the incense of gasoline. He tugs the rope and it starts first time—

a small miracle of the suburbs—and a blue puff of exhaust dissolves
into his jeans. He's got a red bandanna around his neck and 50s cowboy style
pulls it over his nose and mouth as the dry lawn ascends in an amber haze.
Following the mower back and forth, humming, gliding along, he's careless
of everything around him—cars clattering down the street, me standing here
all this time like some burglar casing the joint as the old films have it,
though there's nothing here really worth the effort.
                                             The point is his life
right now is worth it, doing reasonably what needs to be done. He's happy
for a Saturday, the grey peace of early fall, glad for this flat wedge of land
picked up cheap before everyone discovered real estate and mutual funds.
He kills the engine, grabs the bamboo rake for clippings. I'm comparing
our bear-like slump and short legs as he bends over; and standing back up
a little too fast, I feel a lightness, the clouds ascending in my head . . . .

He looks over. Must have known I was here all along. His eyes shine
a brighter green, but I know them like I know the sky—their squint
toward the far tops of the trees. Then he's grinning our crooked front teeth,
smiling like he knows me, a wide smile as if I were some relative gone
twenty years as far as New Jersey or East Jesus and just come back.
Embarrassed, I start walking down the street, and leaning on his rake
he waves an arm, then he's waving both arms crazily over his head,
jumping up once or twice, calling out as I turn the corner and disappear . . . .

                                              for Gerald Stern

Poem about the Soul: Menorca, Spain

The single engine plane lifts up from San Lluis
above the sun-bleached windsock there and circles
Es Castell. Each day this winter he laps the local air,
six or seven wide slow loops, hanging on the under
carriage of a cloud as we look up after it and the trailing
contralto threading the singed evening sky. Higher,
a jet's red contrails scar the irradiant blue which remains
the sole province of Esteban Murillo, his true unworldly
subject which lifted him a level in the world higher
than the still lives of saints. Higher still, the invisible
galaxies blaze blindly away, red-shifted toward the empty
space of space . . .
           Cloud remnants scatter clock-like
about the sun, and the plane, like a rusty second hand,
passes over the humming line of roofs, the fused black
branches of the palms.
           Out here, I feel there's something
I've forgotten—name, address, directions on the dresser
left among wadded bills and change, in a city so far back
I can barely see the brown exhausted afternoon drift
over the wide sidewalks and turtle-back sedans, someone
in shirt sleeves and tie leaning from a window above
the Rexall Drug, reading want ads for a city to the west.
Yellow stoplight sagging on a wire at the corner
of a five-floor walk up—there's a full tank of gas
in the Oldsmobile, and he goes . . .
           I walked out here
pockets empty except for a lucky piece from Canada
saved at the cold end of my 45th year—a Loon, a half bright
hard metal dollar intended to approximate gold. It's as close
to gold as it is to luck. All the same, I walk along and whistle
tunes the air waves would have carried to the old radio
on that dresser—"My Blue Heaven" or "I've Got The World
On A String." Late 40s blithe romance and 50s upbeat impossibility,

a mix so I keep the ironies in play, so I can remember my father
in his brown slacks and tasseled suede shoes, so I remember
not to expect things like a kid in Woolworth's in 1952.
All of this reminding me that I'm not even 45 anymore
and am wearing some other man's coat, a once snazzy houndstooth
tweed I snagged in the charity shop. It goes with jeans, and
was only $4.00, which saves those wadded bills for a menú del día,
one of the amazing three-course lunches which, for six bucks,
keep body and soul together all day—so I'm lucky after all.

****

It can't just be the sun I'm after here, not in winter, not all
this way? Rather, the long term effect is what I want
to know about—how terminal is it? Leaning on my rented balcony,
I pronounce the precepts of two languages against the wind,
and what does it get me? Not one inch closer to the clouds
than rent money already has—not grace or insight nor reprieve
from the self-important past. Only the slim notion of a feeling
now that might sustain me despite this Tramontana wind
descending from the north with its jack hammer breath.
And I can take that, the scouring of the backdrop here
in the middle of the sea. Anywhere else, we're ruining
the sky like there's no tomorrow—Los Angeles, the Amazon,
the faces of men and beasts eaten away by the sour air
in Athens, the arms of caryatids so frail they can't hold
their own hands up let alone the porticos of cataleptic gods.

We're at the mercy of the light, the plants breathing out
our breath—stop that and no one questions the first invisible
thing. We're not going into the sky, not going anywhere
but back to the enduring dull compounds of dust. This pearl-rich
winter sky might be something though, some sample of the form
it took to fix one life firmly within another? This sky
over the Mediterranean blown clear, beeswax bright—
I let it coat my palms, holding them up for the final gloss
skinning the blue edge of the pines.

36

                    And I have to ask myself,
as the famous wind prevails, as bleached laundry across
the rooftops flails arms and legs, as the waves whip up
and overrun a white fishing skiff until it barely glimmers
back its opaque shape from the glass-blue bottom of the cove,
what has already taken the past and added it to the dark
without looking back to see if someone might be standing
on a cliff trying to strike a match, or turning on his lamp
by the chair to read Lao-tzu or Charles Péguy's riddles
in support of God, or even pouring out a small glass of fino
to measure the bronze horizon line?
                              In the esplanada,
in the streets, a hundred kids are waiting for sundown—
two to a motorbike, smoking in groups on the street corners
like something from the 50s. Like them, why should I care
if the plane keeps going around the small sky of San Lluis
like a lost planet? Only this: that it comes down with grace
and with the dark so that they may go about unknown
into the unknown with the one blessing of the night.
But I am consoled so long as I hear that high murmur
plying the apparent nothing above us, burning in the cold
climate there that it climbs continually to know.

                            ****

And the line of old men without a boat, or a job on one
anymore, who sit on the stone bench cut into the cliff
of Cala Corb, they also pay the plane no mind and do not
look to the sky with questions. They keep their regular
positions each day until the sun goes. It is easy to look
at them and make a case for the sleeping collective soul
as they speak to each other or to the sea, gesturing
as if they were still untangling the nets or testing wind.
Other than the sea, most have never been off the island.
Not going. All the death and life and rain falling from this
only sky, falling, as they see it, in the acknowledged
democracy of wind. For all intents and purposes, they know

what's coming, are content to offer themselves this light,
hoard it within as they walk home, holding it in
their empty hands. Enough of this, enough days among
enough friends and perhaps you grow calm, never lose it—
the luster never goes altogether from you?
                                        Near the window
I slice some lemon into a glass and cover the luminous
rind with an ounce of dark Cynar, that dense liquor
distilled from the artichoke, a drink that holds
the same burnt color as that relic of the saint's tongue
on a spike. I think too of the thistle and its black seeds,
the half-bitter essence igniting in me like a slow fuse.
I think of the small plane easing down to land, the old
engine shaped like a thistle flower, a crown of grease
and oil sparking, keeping it burning, bright enough to fly.

                                ****

I remember Fellini saying, "Sometimes pulling a little tail,
one finds an elephant at the other end." And so while life
turns out glorious in bits, impossible in stages, imponderable
finally at the one level above sorrow which we all want
to know, we breathe and hope we are not deceived by the music
of the trees, the reeds strung with rain, the unscripted stars
we cannot escape. For one thing, the pointed hats, the wings
and silver replications of the moon are all taken in at the end.
For another, that road along the sea where the procession and
makeshift band turned back is the same one you set out on,
thinking of the ten thousand things you would have out there
among the lights.
                        Federico was laid in state high in front of the azure
sky from his last film: angels in coveralls and painters' caps
going about up there, touching up the background, a full orchestral
arrangement of clouds indicating perhaps a city of white aspirations
above all the visible poverty of the grass and unpaved lanes.
And here, by the shore, the sea churns away and articulates
a silence never found when gone into the wilderness or

onto the high roofs at dawn. You look west into the white fire of the sky, and a small plane disappears, a pinpoint in the sun.

Death of the Poet, 1936

I don't want to hear again that the dead do not lose their blood . . .

—Federico Garcia Lorca

Despite the black fuse ticking in the blood,
the days like fine ash sifting sunward
through our atoms and the weak theory of flesh,
despite the clear cloud of the soul hovering
like a late afternoon moon over the hills of the past,
and a wind dictating its deep songs through
the sorrowful postures of the elms,
who ever stands up, detached as starlight,
as the great lies of great fiction,
and with philosophy calmly drinks the cold cup
of his own death—the immediate future
a fusillade of bullets, comets biting out black
space and time, the only signal to the landscape
a fogged breath, staggered and homeless as a cloud?

Who doesn't come to morning with some hope
shining on his shirt sleeves, not of course like a star,
but at least like an old scar burning on the body
of the will, like a little gleam from an old coin
rubbed across a white cuff, and there,
in that moment, doesn't embrace some shred of belief
in the timelessness of his bones, in the essential power
of his two shaking hands to cup water and lift
the first gift of the earth to his face and see
that face still shining there against the sky—
or the power of his voice, its influences
of rivers and green seas, to still call the hours
to order like the strings of the guitar and be
acknowledged along the avenues and in cafes?

Who could imagine the hive of the mind, its blue
electricity spinning to a stop even as the eyes
proclaim the fire-fed tributaries of dawn?

No one. Not one of us in the ordinary assignments of our lives,
for, doing what little we can, what does it matter
when the knock at the door comes for the wrong reason,
for the dark heart of reason, or no reason, really, at all?
Dioscoro Galindo Gonzalez, schoolmaster and republican,
beloved by his students, but denounced as a "dangerous enemy"
by a secretary to the local municipal corporation.
Joaquin Arcollas Cabezas and Francisco Galadi Melgar,
minor bullfighters and anarchists, "undesirables"
delivered to the Black Squad—those boys from the Catholic
middle class, sons of merchants, lawyers, bankers
who had *carte blanche* to butcher "reds."
These citizens were driven out the road to Alfacar in darkness
while Manuel de Falla wept in his moonless courtyard
and listened to the stars fall without music,
the firing from the cemetery in Granada going on
in small bursts through the early hours of morning.
Near the spring Fuente Grande the assassins shot
their victims and rolled the bodies into the olive groves
on the right hand side of the road as you come from Viznar:
two bullfighters, a schoolmaster with a wooden leg,
one in a white shirt with a loose artistic tie.

There is no reason to forget. Not 60 years.
Not the Alhambra with its amusing gardens
and mosaics. Not the coach tours to the gypsy caves
nor the one fine restaurant beneath the aqueduct.
Not Socialism or the EEC. His father did not forget.
He took the extortion note they forced him to write—
a request for a donation of 1,000 pesetas to the army—
into exile in New York, where for the last nine years
of his life, he carried it in his wallet—the final thing
the poet ever wrote.

Let us say more than Fate,
Falangists, or even Franco and fascism. Let us say
Ramon Ruis Alanzo, junior officer who acted
"on his own initiative" arresting the poet for,
among other things, broadcasting to the Russians
on a secret radio. Let us say Juan Luis Trescastro,
accomplice of Ruis Alanzo, who boasted the next morning
of helping at the execution, of firing "Two bullets
in his arse for being a queer." Also Gov. Valdez,
who claimed the poet was already taken off
when the documents for his release were produced
and he was still in custody upstairs. And Gen. Quipe de Llano,
commander of the Nationalists in Andalusia, who, over the phone,
gave his dark code: "Give him coffee, plenty of coffee."

And let us not forget the bourgeoisie of Granada
who ground that coffee, who face to face, executed
well over 2,000 of their countrymen and -women
to eliminate left wing opposition—doctors, professors,
town councilors, schoolmasters, workers and trade unionists.
And who did so with gusto, terror, and the great moral certainty
of the right, who rang bells, kept their saints' days, gave to the church,
and lived out their lives comfortably denying everything.

In the blue clay of the barranca of Viznar, five bad miles of road
to the north, the dead were shoveled into shallow graves.
Later pines were planted to cover the mounds and hollows,
to erase the few stones placed there. Later still,
Franco ordered the trees cut and the ground leveled
to make that place invisible to those who kept coming.
But he could not dismiss the sparrows who hung on like remorse,
unseen in the olives and roadside pines, confabulating like ghosts
in low clouds. He could not stop the fine grit of salt
falling in the steady accusation of wind.

42

He sleeps his sleep of apples, each with its small lock
of light, the sleep of the ocean, moonlight dissolving
into it. He sleeps with that gold on his lips and hears
nothing of the torments of the reeds or the dead child,
his mouth of water beneath a white camellia
that has become the moon. He dreams the dream
of the mountain beyond the valley of rain,
and does not hear the long silence continue to issue
from the windows of the state. He does not see the blind
white eyes of dawn as each day the birds bear witness
from the bloody stars of their throats.

4 Benches, 14 Orange Trees

I'm watching the old men on these 4 back-to-back
slat benches, beneath 7 pairs of Valencia orange trees
spaced so a green air infuses the 2 pedestrian streets
that join here for the square in Mahon. It is instructive, and,
to some degree reassuring—they've known each other since
they could first sing out down these stone streets,
though in truth they look as if they've always been old,
as if they remember the Carthaginians and the Moors.
And listening to them I hear what could be a bit of both
spun on the choppy syntax and swallowed vowels—
the undercurrent of Old French, Catalán cutting Spanish down to size.
Their rhythms and repetitions make a music out of morning—
4 or 5 crowding a bench, on the edge, facing 1 who stands
to lecture, commanding a rhetoric that appeals to clouds
and is supported by the fierce birds of his hands.

They have given up cigars, have listened darkly and at length
to doctors, something the younger men dismiss lighting up
in banks, restaurants, buses, jewelry stores—at all times
and everywhere asserting themselves in smoke and neglect
as if life and death did not apply. Not these old ones.
They cherish this little place to congratulate each other
on the weather, the lack of wind, on continuing to breathe,
comfortable in the citrus scented hours. They did their work,
that's done—hands thick as slabs of bacon tell you that.

And work, I think, is not the subject, they have moved to art,
the democratic crafts of greeting, praising the day in 5 salutations.
They love to stop someone and grasp both hands, pat the shoulder
until the litany is complete. The same when one of them leaves
for his afternoon's soup and squid—waves and salutes across the square,
"deos" for "adiós" or half a dozen other ways to sing goodbye.
They've paid the price of the fields or sea in full
so that they may enjoy their idea of gentlemanly apparel:

cardigans in green or brown, rayon dress shirts, ties in muted stripes,
pressed flannel slacks with cuffs. You'd swear each was doing well
in business for himself somewhere in Ohio in 1958. And so
if an orange falls, they ignore it and go on gesturing to heaven
or the empty sky, or empty heaven—go on filling the square
with their half songs and agreements, proclaiming the dozen
truths anyone should know. Having arrived at this station
in life—indicated by such sartorial splendor—a collective pride
does not allow stooping to windfall fruit.

All morning
they are here, doing nothing for as long as the air holds out,
happy despite a good part of everything behind them, gone down
that country road where dust catches in daylight and smudges
out the blue a bit, where once the heavy wagons cut ruts across
this flat table of stone. And they know that the road's end
is out there—they hear the rag man with his cart coming
and quickly close their shutters on the street and his calls,
returning to the dim kitchen for another coffee, to the small
courtyard where one canary is still singing for the sun.

At the end of these trees, a street lamp holds a white halo
against the sky, but I'm not sitting beneath it working out
the square root of wisdom nor have I arrived here in my youth
ready to rebuild a land of crumbling walls. No, I go unnoticed
in my jeans, and sport coat from the charity shop across the way.
I could be any one not at work this day, or taking the 11:00 break
for café and ensaimades, so casual is a business day anyway
which pauses over 3 hours each afternoon.

I'm taking account
of half my life is all, grateful for the time out, this sky's clean slate
in front of me, the disinclination here to figure out final sums.
I'm thinking of friends far to the west who still meet 40 years later
at the breakwater to fish where a line has no chance of reaching
past the waves—talking, as they used to say, just to hear themselves talk.
Mechanics, lawyers, bread truck drivers—what can it matter now?
20 years in academia and there's no job important enough to ruin your heart
by middle age. To be almost happy now, I need only look 3 feet above

45

my head to the fruit hanging half gold, half green, or a little higher
to the constant sun and keep breathing as evenly. I want to see Murillo's
"St. Francis In The Kitchen of The Angels" and know again what it takes
to feed a soul on only mist and stone. I am trying to take a little lesson
from these leaves blown both ways and coming back calmly to themselves.

****

But damn, Burt Lancaster has died! I leave the country once
every 10 years and this is the kind of thing that happens. ZAM,
just like that. I only saw the headline in a Spanish movie tabloid:
BURT LANCASTER MUERTO. Not a clue. He must have had some
good years left. But who ever knows all the factors working against you—
silent as air in an island cove no one is breathing?
Look away for a minute and things go sailing over the edge.

How does it all add up? For example, the coats in the charity shop
in Mahon are the same ones found in Fresno or Philadelphia—
world-wide someone's got his hand in it all, keeps an eye out,
has distribution, contacts and associates, knows who does tweed
in Ireland, serge in Toledo, decides about the brown polyester pinstripe,
the grey worsted with large red checks, the hounds tooth, the gabardine,
and how everyone without real money will have to sport these
mild atrocities new and second hand for close to 50 years.

So who was taking care of business then when Burt went out?
He never flinched. And lightning, fire, thunder, who ever grinned
that many teeth as completely in malice, knowledge or reckless joy?
And hell, Burt had religion to boot. To believe in the longevity of desire,
you only had to hear him—in his 60s then—in *Atlantic City* as he recited
the ritual of Susan Sarandon's bathing, the rinsing of arms, breasts,
and neck with soap flakes and lemon after her shift at the seafood bar.
There are people who'd bury bodies under football stadiums for that
kind of eloquence and fervor. In *1900* he didn't hesitate a second
to put his 2 bare feet squarely into cow shit to make the scene between

46

the patron and the peasant girl work. With reason and patience
he taught a kid to cook garlic shrimp, a sparrow to have the fortitude
of a prize fighter. On the beach in black & white he loved Deborah Kerr
as no one ever would again. I even bought him in the bad westerns
and war films which were all, in the 50s, Hollywood decided we would watch.

Who can we look to now to stick his chin squarely out at fate and duck
its long left hook? Jack Lemon, Kirk Douglas, Tom Cruise?
True enough, there's still Tony Quinn who has the charisma
in one hand to give a story life or a life a story by just raising
that hand carefully to the sky, knowing what a dicey thing a soul can be.
He has the power but not the glory according to the number crunchers,
not the rating anymore to land a leading role. Word is, he's trying
to get a film off the ground on his own—Tolstoy at the end where
he finds religion, or rather *is* religion—starting his own church,
going about the countryside on a train, his car turned into a chapel,
coming to the window in the white tunic weighed down with gold thread,
mystical until death as the snowfall light spinning over the black firs.
Burt began in film noire, in *The Killers*—by the end he knew what was
coming for him, but was clear, sure, calm, and always came back.

****

There is still life ahead—ample perhaps, gregarious or serene
at a simple level, as these men in Mahon—all who have outlived
Burt Lancaster—demonstrate who do not need these lovely oranges
from the trees of Valencia. If I put the pressure and ambition
behind me, I could well make do with an orange for each pocket
of my coat, a free, small space to breathe, figuring I have
maybe 40 years left if I retreat to the provinces, drink and eat
with moderation the fruits of the earth thereby remaining
on the earth.

　　　　Counting, that's what I've been doing. Obsessive,
spinning like this globe, heart in a cage, Type-A, trying to read
every schedule of the air, get there first or finally. A pocket full

of paper confetti, that's all—throw it into the wind. And what was it
that took Burt? Too much work, high/hard living, stroke or heart?
Sure, all of the above. Star exploding, nova in the small galaxy
of the cells, which, for all practical purposes is where all
those stars are anyway. Flash. Then, against the dark, that nothing
that every bit of worry finally amounts to, plays back—reel to
reel—a life as you knew it in time before the blind and
seemingly unmarked distance dissolving beyond the trees.

Morning, Dreaming of Empire

Es Castell, Menorca, Spain

October, the tourists gone back to Manchester and the north
and I command this cliff-top tower, risking a third cup of decaf,
chocolate biscuit on the side.
　　　　　　　　Ocean liners cruise in, freighters
disappear on a string of smoke, and soon, the Spanish Navy
will circle the harbor in its war surplus boat, assuring us
that the Communists have still not come ashore.
　　　　　　　　　　　Later, I'll salute
the fishing fleet, a procession of gulls littering the air behind them,
their irreverent hosannas to the fruits of the sea rising
on the chop and wake—may they all find the bounty
that was once the sea, all that was bequeathed to them
beneath the sky.
　　　　　　In my royal blue jogging suit, I'm out
to feed the cats above the cove—noblesse oblige—where I am known
for my Friskies and common touch, acknowledged by stone chats
and the five-colored finch, the wind that's made its bed in crowns
of olive trees and broom. I nod to neighboring kingdoms of loquat
and oleander, the walled gardens of gold hibiscus and palm.
I stop to shake the stones from my shoe—envy and its carping heart,
the inscrutable bequests of fate.
　　　　　　　　　Here, I am almost light, clear,
unburdened as the island air that allows lichens to breathe, bright
as turmeric in their starry clusters across the rocks. I might even give up
the eminent domain of mail, the burn and festering, the waiting
for a wholly, white, improbable circumstance—the envelopes
always sent out on the backs of sea turtles. Too often, I've found myself
pacing the square, the resin scent of the pines like a little methedrine
as I peek through the barred windows of the post office to the slots—
all the mice racing in the maze.
　　　　　　　　　But letters that haven't arrived
in twenty years will not come now: The Rockefeller Center offering
their villa by the lake, small staff and cellar of modest wines

49

in support of a work in progress; Gotham House Books accepting,
enthusiastically, a three-movie contract thrown into the deal;
"The Today Show" requesting I appear for a Mexican cooking bit
with Bryant Gumbel which will distinguish me once and for all
from that other fellow with my name still wearing his father's
school tie and blazer, at his usual mid-town table for lunch.
Or Stanford offering a Chair targeted for a white, middle-aged male
lacking celebrity, correct theoretical views—one who is well meaning
up to the fourth drink.
                              Am I alone in feeling the world tugging
at my shirt sleeve regardless of what solitude I pursue, however beaten
off the far map? Will I only shake loose of a hundred minor defeats
when I become as ambitionless as clouds?
                                          Two hundred miles out
in the Mediterranean, in the absolute dark, I reflect on the unpublished
mind of the stars, all that light and lost meaning passing by—no way
to get ahead now, get a handle on all that spin. I cannot rule the waves.

Something rusted, sticking up from the sand some day might explain
the relegation to the provinces, the soul as boat beached on that spiny shore.
But how can I complain when I think of Po Chu-I sent up river
hundreds of years ago to govern a province so small and far from court
that no one heard when he fell ill staring down the vacant
corridors of the sky.
                        What good working your life away without one outcome
as reasonable as the continuing resolution passed by these old men
in the square as they breathe through each tin-bright morning,
in allegiance to nothing more than sun and the ontology of trees,
where there is just enough melody in the boughs to carry your hopes
into another day?
                    The string arrangement of the sea underscores
my proclivity for that refined city of air wherein all the princely estates
of this profession take hold. But these aspirations only match
the echo of each wave rising off the rocks, salt and sea foam
and the abbreviated *extravagaria* of the light, the wind insisting
I need to reassess—given anything I might point to from here,
I've been singing all along for whatever singing alone is worth.

                                          for Gary Soto

IV

Astronomy Lesson: at Café Menorca

I have just asked for stars—and wine from a region
where grapes are not clustered in remorse. I want to speak
    as elegantly as the sun-struck sentences of fish shifting
in the cove, but here I sit in my coat, crumpled and mute
    as a cloud—old troubles traveling the small distances of salt
and pepper, elbows alone eloquent with the shine of tables,
    acknowledged by dust from one establishment to the next
as I point skyward at the fiery crests of local birds.
    Aquí están las estrellas Señor. And a plate is set before me
with pastries and creme caramels, a spiral galaxy sugared
    with light. *Pero, estoy triste*—I cannot recall the words
for light, for clouds, cannot place an order for rain
    deep and green as under the trees of childhood, or for a sky—
el cielo—reflecting both faces of the sea—*blanco y azul*—
    or for the first planets white as soap flakes above the bay.
¿Algo más Señor? Something stronger perhaps? I try again
    asking for brandy, one with the courage of fire, and a *café*
con limón, without the rind of laughter that edges the dark.
    ¿Es más tarde—es todo Señor? No, I'd also like the glass wrapper
my heart arrived in from the sky, and add whatever advice
    the wind can offer on living far from home. *Por favor, Señor,*
es más tarde, the help is sad—even the stars here are overworked.

Old Light

The universe is ordered—it's just not personal . . .
not like us, or art, both its constructions, out to explain
it all beside a sea as smooth as a polished baby grand—
a sprinkling of evening stars, sonatinas, a finished,
as far as we can tell, symphony—
                              everything seen
in a halo of meaning.   A third of the constellation
of the brain devoted to processing light as it travels through
to the cortex, where we enter memory,
                              in black & white . . .
doves breaking in a galvanized scrum and gloss, where you
lift your hand up after them on the back porch in Montecito,
stiff as cardboard in your First Communion suit
where the daylight's just jumped out of you—what template
of photons from your bones and skin
                              fixed you
apparently forever in two dull tones? What moves through us
that *is* us, holds that glint off the Pontiac in the drive,
that blinding star of the hood ornament igniting the snapshot?
Those fishbone clouds, white tines, brush strokes across the azure
reaches of the west—those clay-grey clouds over a canyon
echoing your absence that far away.

                    X-rays, infrared,
ultraviolet, ordinary daylight—it's all the same note
played at different speeds.   Microwaves, background radiation
of the Big Bang, the oldest light in the universe hums away unseen.
Still, after fifteen billion years, start-up galaxies pop
on the photo plates like flash bulbs of the paparazzi, a blue-
veined glossy milt crawling the cosmic vault.

                                        Beyond ourselves,
what have we been looking for so far, all this time?
Magritte said the invisible is something
that light cannot throw light upon.
                                        We've sliced
millions of light years deep into the holographic dark
to find that galaxies form in filaments, a filigree about the void
as if we'd cut across some glistening soap bubble froth,
but this doesn't come close to the long range question
of the soul every Pre-Socratic posed elementally at the edge
of the Aegean.
                        But closer to home, what sustains
that fugitive filament glowing in the eyes of men all night
in the Eagle Cafe? What's the unreplenished source for that?
The white gravy and chicken-fried steak, the nebulae of grease
floating on coffee in the bone-thick mugs, the fluorescent bulbs
shining almost out into the deserted parking lot?
                                        No, but
there's a refraction, a greasy X smudged on your white shirtsleeve,
branding you with the past, with dust—the same thing.

Look. What else have we got? Arguably, we're the light's
best evidence among the rocks and twigs. Our problem then
is how to keep it from going, behaving part and particle
like everything else in a universe guttering, it would seem,
toward some dark?
                        The least of us have a little of it, even if it's dull
as unpolished silverware or the smeared center of a cloud,
the bright oxygen of the brain thinning to a tinfoil grey.

Each morning crows report above the oaks like stars
reversed out against a white sky—black marks against the heart,
a bit of certainty skimmed off the earth's silver edge.
No matter what part of loss you offer them—the stars, the crows—
they will not have it, will not carry it off beyond the dawn-blue hills,
and there is just this small splendor left in all that they refuse—
your breath, a little mist escorted by the sky.

                                              I hope it is true
what we have said in darkness and in hope—that we're essentially
and at long last light, and when we come to it and come apart,
are all fulgent strings, some everlasting lustrous chord,
and not Presbyterians in stern collars and long black gowns,
and not more dust—
                      but instead reflect a sparkling
sea green, that damask rose and violet resonant after centuries
of smoke and soot has been scraped from the Sistine ceiling
to reveal the sheer agenda of light in the Michelangelo sky.

Winter: No. 7 Miranda de Cala Corb

Sorrows—how we waste them!
—Rilke

Light blown beneath the epaulets of cloud, mute alphabet of birds
          underlining morning's wet slate—those clouds racing, gathering up
all we've forgotten, all we ever were, chalked up and carried off
          in the custody of wind. Fate comes to little more now than rain,
the galvanized, the glimmering sorrows you would somehow put to use.
          Whatever else is coming—numb shiver of afternoon, sea mist
dim as a sanded shard of glass—you waited for these empty hours
          like no one else, and they arrived to find you drifting
like a gull between two layers of blue, second hand and dependent
          on any mercy of sun. All the world's fresh air going by,
reminding your cells to breathe, to settle a manic heart, its stray dog doubt.
          You're not getting beyond the washed-out blue in front of you,
the problem of how to fill in that blank without turning to another
          pale imitation of the past—the pigeons reeling in their panicked loops
above the pines. The sky is finally the best place to leave regrets—
          wheeling as purposelessly as those birds. So, say this to the wind:
say, *Swell.* You're satisfied with everything—the doctrinaire chorus of stars,
          the indeterminate blessings of a diminished dusk-edged dome.
And there's no problem killing time as the heavens work up another arrangement
          in the outer provinces of light and dust—the end of space
streaming off right in front of your eyes. But who hasn't looked there hoping
          to outlast the industry of the dark as the world floats by
singed with crimson and aquamarine above the woodblock sky, the invisible
          boundary of your breath burning there where we feel sure
we deserve something more than our lives? I came here for something.
          But after days spent overlooking an irresolute sea, counting
sun-cut white caps that surrender to nothing, I forgot for a while exactly
          what that was—and this, it seems, is what I wanted all along.

Why I Am Not Yet a Zen Master

"I keep going to meetings where no one's there,
And contributing to the discussion . . ."
                                        —Larry Levis

What can you do? So much horseshit on the wind. A pitiful gloss
of less and less, a line of winter leaves, window-level against the dusk,
shining briefly as those silver wings on the helmets of Mercury dimes

which once stood for speed, or inspiration, and which have all passed
now, into the solemn amnesia of the 50s, into the dark
drawers of coin shops in the abandoned steel towns of Pennsylvania.

And, one of those dimes, no doubt, like our last best effort,
lies with the lint left in the pocket of the professor's grey slacks,
the one who has tabled every resolution for light for the last forty years.

How can I respond as calmly as the bow's one reverberating string?
How side-step The President's Panel for Obfuscation, avoid the moth-eaten
clouds loitering over the hills, the trustees of those redundant hills
likewise in their brown and useless suits?
                                        It's no longer enough
to have the horse sense to sit incommunicado as those clouds
while the dialogue between the ivy and the brick goes on.
Let the able-bodied go free, considering the lateness of the hour . . . .

You can pray for the amendment of the dark coming over the roof slates
like Genghis Khan and his colleagues, scourging even the sleeping grass.

You may manage one or two addenda to the old furniture of the heart,
a scratch or two against the faltering realms of breath—one sentence
which shifts like wind across the sand dunes of the Sahara,
as the Committee for the Imponderable takes another straw poll.

No one will give ground, acknowledge the unimportance of East Jesus State
in certain relation to the monograph of arteries and skin unthreading
like the elbow of an old tweed coat, the leaves beyond the bookcase
with a *memento mori* about the end of things always as close as the air,
a vacancy absolute in the industrial sky, that breeze leaving a residue
of tin on your tongue . . . .
                              I want to walk out spiritually
incognito in my street clothes and cap, one among the working crowd
crossing The Walt Whitman Bridge and stop mid span, mid air,
as invisible above the rush-hour and steaming stacks as everything
leaving Philadelphia for the uninhabited sky, and contribute my thought
about the bent wheel of work, proclaim one last democratic vista,
even if it's only the Pine Barrens of south Jersey.
                                        But next to the windowpane,
my memory stalls in the dust-hooked corners and replays a news clip
in glorious black and white—the UN with Khrushchev and his shoe, shouting
the solution in his bad suit, "We will bury you."
                                        Bless me, oh Lord, if only
among the burnt air and salt-brown needles, the sea, and flat expanse
of acidic soil.
                 May we one day reason as surely as dune grass against a gale,
before we lie down among the dead armor of the horseshoe crabs
proclaiming their rigid text forever to the ebb tide and themselves.

May we praise the sea birds skimming the spindrift and the waves,
the free verses of wind in their arms.
                                  If I ascend to anything,
it will be yellow leaves hanging through autumn, the air there allowing
the trees to speak as if the past added up to anything more than the sediment,
the dust, the words that will one day block our hearts . . . .
                                        I aspire no higher
than the star pine and its ladder-even boughs from where everything thins
into that valley beyond our eyes,
                              where there is always, it seems, the white
page of a kite, straining high on a string . . . . I should make something of it,

write down the minutes for the last meeting of lost souls. I should let it go
into the altitudes and the unknown, a small lesson silence lives by.

20 Years of Grant Applications & State College Jobs

"Why, without theory there is no meaning."
—former colleague at a committee meeting

All I want now is a small dirt patio beneath two or three pines,
maybe one palm glittering with dates, one lemon sapling in a terra-cotta pot
standing for hope. A place where I can return to my scholarship of the sky,
re-establish a franchise with the sun. A place—I swear—where I will leave
most of the talking to the trees and purple finches, where I am at last renowned
among sparrows for my philosophy of crumbs.
                              A place where I walk out
each day at 8:00 or 9:00 to appraise the likelihood of daylight advancing
beyond the cool green efforts of the boughs, where I set my coffee
and unread newspaper down on the metal table—a round one, the size
of a trash can lid, just big enough for wine and glasses, a basket of bread—
one painted that thick civic green like those in the sidewalk cafes
and parks in Paris—my last concession to a sentimental education.

I won't mind that the paint's chipped or that salt air eats away the legs;
I will praise the fog, its long beggar's coat dragging in from Point Conception
like some lost uncle in an Ingmar Bergman film. I will praise the tiny ranch-
style house the color of fog, my luck to end up in Lompoc, the last place
on the California coast almost no one wanted. I will refold the paper,
my notes scrawled in the margins where I've tried again to locate
the trace elements of God.
                              To feel industrious, I'll get to my feet
about 11:00 and spray the hose around to keep down the dust—
a bit extra for the lantana lining the flagstones to the door,
a bit more for the aloe vera, the pomegranate, their blossoms aflame.
Every so often, I'll rake the patches of pine needles into a pile,
but before I decide where to move them next, a gust rearranges them
with an abstract but even hand.
                              What will I care,
sitting in my rain bleached chair, one leg tapping the shade, the other
going to sleep in the sun, content to stare at my hot-pink hibiscus

slowly ascending the stucco wall? After 20 years, what can it matter
how long it takes to burn its way up the glistening air?
Even the stars are wearing down without a thought for us,
unattainable all this time. That should have been a lesson long ago . . . .

I hereby resign all pretenses to the astronomy of New York—
appointments, invitations, awards, the genius grants.
Whenever the phone doesn't ring, it's them.
I'll settle for this wooden gate, a gravel drive announcing friends
who arrive for walks, for the Zinfandel and dish of Spanish olives;
friends who remember the sea, how good it was 20 years ago,
loose as driftwood in our lives, to have nothing and happily
drink that green, hard Chablis each evening by the Pacific
thinking we would have that light.
                                                        Now, I love the grey
and ragtag gulls whose hoots and aggravation betray their finds—
all that chance deserves. So after our walk, we're satisfied
just sitting outside, a Pavarotti aria holding off death,
drifting out the kitchen window onto the ambered light.

And what can we make of the Maya now? Their lost tongue,
their psalms of stone? They disappeared in the middle
of setting it all down and no one missed them for centuries.
And what was behind the anonymous workers of the Nazca Plains,
scraping off the desert's scrofulous skin for images of animals
and some politico's son, lines so long they only make sense from the sky—
and none of us birds?
                                        Whose administrative mission was that?
100 years and the job will still be there. How good now to say Good-bye
to that arrogance which asks if there can be meaning
without first arranging the padded folding chairs of theory.

I'd like to apply for my life. I want the Guggenheim
to give me back my good will, the ease—no, the joy—
I once carried around with me, going down the street
in uncertainty, not enough gas in the tank to get out of town.
But I'll settle for this unpopular valley of fog, cholla flats and sand,

the occasional breeze thumbing my book, humming a blue line.
I'll take a small patio of unglamorous old dirt, a few pines
speaking simply in the resinous language of the only world
there is, immediate and meaningful as your next breath.
I'll praise the uneventful afternoon, and accept the wind
applauding in the silver dollar eucalyptus as my reward.

for Gary Soto, Jon Veinberg, & Gary Young

Against Theory

Es Castell, Menorca

Out here, I can say anything.
        —Larry Levis

Once, I want to go somewhere and offer no proof I'm there—
no post cards, no reports on my research into an average day
of breathing beside the palms and bougainvillea, among dust
and dry weeds, alongside the field larks. I don't want to acknowledge
my insignificance in the face of nothing beyond the sea,
or be compared to the fields of thistles closing calmly with evening
around their blue hearts . . . .
                    Half the world away, even more reason
for the Foundations not to notice, so I'm appealing to the pine trees
for support, for inspiration to the salt air my skin remembers
and the fog of the past through which meaning still enters.
                                    I like
the Sardinian Warbler who knows his mind amid gorse or pittosporum,
his own voice well enough to keep at it regardless of red kites and tourists
dropping all summer high out of the blue, content to proclaim
his warm blood above the historical stones—who knows he is all
he has against an unambiguous dark.
                            In the flat below, the retired barber
trims his razor-straight mustache—every day at 4:30 "It's Rumba Time!"
Forty years after the fact, who's he kidding, mixing a shaker of Manhattans
maraca-like to that hip-bumping beat—maybe only, or not even, himself?
But who else is there finally to please? No one there to tell him otherwise
as he turns up Xavier Cugat, and saves his life.
                                I accept evening
without a hermeneutics of the light. What I want is to write what I want—
and now, why not tell the truth? There is no other word for Death—
no *discourse* is going to revise that.
                        A stone chat knows the significance
of air, but little, it seems, about those not privileged with wings—

it must be a structuralist, or late humanist, and like me it's likely
he will not be promoted beyond the sky, and will continue to wade
through low clouds with his unmitigated aspirations.

                                               Likewise,
I admire the feral cats, their deconstruction of fish. I understand myself
speaking to these few small souls in the republic of scraps,
these godly scroungers who know my voice from the local boys'
with their rocks rehearsed on strings, boys I curse from my window
in Spanish and in English, and come away questioning the essential
text of pity which even children have abandoned.

                                            So I'm questioning
souls in the first place, anything more abstract than the stars, though
I confess I have too often relied on stars, their obscure grace,
their irreproachable light.

                                  It's clearer each time the fishing boats
lumber in from the intractable sea, gulls whirling behind them
as if spun in a huge invisible cage, the zinc-white hulls appearing
to flake away on the air, bits of themselves spun out, trailing,
going to pieces in the wind.

                                I find myself at the cliff
with dry food or sardines, or at the square coveting the elemental
knowledge of the trees, the modest ambition of doves laddering
sun-topped boughs, the desire of swifts to turn the next corner of air
with an unrestrained joy skimmed from a world that will end.

Against the Blue

Es Castell, Menorca

To become a Saint do nothing.
— Shih Shu

Out here at the point, my mind eases, idling
in low gear like the fishing boats lugging in,
throttling down as they hit the harbor buoys—
a little brass propeller spinning below the dark
level of the sea . . . .
                              Whatever conclusions I came to
must have gone off with the Tramontana,
that wind that can blow the paint off buildings
and almost clear your heart. Among the wild
marguerites along the shore, how many days
left between the blue and the blue?

It's enough for me that the sail boats come in
against the prevailing wind, still under sail,
doing slowly what they set out to do,
though speed boats blast by them
like there's no tomorrow.
                              I can see now
it's not about speed, but instead the skill,
the gradual good time to get in, to arrive
on the pearl-colored evening mist, working
the white sails, full and gathering them
in at last in both arms as surely as the stories
of how we've survived so far.
                                        Lately,
an east wind picks up around 5:00. Where
does it all blow through to, and where does it stop?
Oh, there's science for that and the satellite view
where we turn up marked red and brown and lost
beneath the clouded swirls, where we are put
in a larger perspective.

I prefer the metaphors
and the drawn-out explanations of the sea
which push against the world and every formulation
of our will. And why, beyond the justification
of our sea blood and our cells, have a will
except to write laments for everything
lost before the sea, and to have the time
to praise those lines when there's little else
you've called for all your life,
and it's come.
                    Isn't it enough
that you were here in the yellow evening,
glistening in your own salt, and the wind
moved one way or the other, and the days held
on long enough for you to breathe the light
worn off the sandstone walls and call
your life your own over the sea kelps
and the fish content in the tides, as if the eyes
that God sees us with demanded any more
than this distracted love.
                    How many saints
have you met? On these dirt paths you have kicked up
the fossils of snails, shells curled white as sea foam,
and after centuries, their pure brains evaporated
into chalk. What differences do you now foresee?
The lake of stars will soon arrive and no one
really finds their way there either.
                    Oh the fox tails
and the burning marguerites gone brown—we are
the wind's past. Much has happened, but it's gone
on the light; still, it's the light that holds us nonetheless
as we hold the world inside our porous brains
with that first idea of light, of salt shining
from the tides—and it turns us flower-like for sun
or bends us in a breeze where we are free
a while to sit and point at the sea or sky
and know just this much against the blue.

Ars Vita

The last island and its inhabitant,
The two alike, distinguish blues,
Until the difference between air
And sea exists by grace alone,
In objects, as white this, white that.
    — Wallace Stevens "Variations on a Summer Day"

Even on an island, anonymous as a wave—the Mediterranean
and all this space and time shifting by—it's still the same
sky at the window, hawk circling in the sun,
same question with its blanks waiting to be filled in.
And there it is—just air. It only carries in your clouds
from farther off, and the clouds puff up like, well,
like clouds, but you can't let things go like that. No,
this is serious business, putting your life piecemeal together.
A few honed bones, whole cloth, and sweet sounds blossom
from a pittosporum hedge just below the apparitional pines—
and Jesus, you will not stop praising the birds. They too
had somber beginnings, like the clouds, dark and in a minor key,
that belly-crawled across Europe's old hills.
                                Now you
prefer the more equatorial view—red macaw running on
in the banana palm, a cigar-gold rum reverberating
its major chords throughout both hemispheres
of the brain, longitudes and meridian, the sun-rubbed
demarcations between old and new dissolving from where you sit.
But it's only the same sequence of neurons firing from bases
of the double helix which brought us up from fish,
and you feel free to fall back as far as you like
to keep the grey globe spinning with sound and sight:
"Moonlight Cocktails," "Old Buttermilk Sky."
                                Or you come up
to speed with atoms, their geodesic domes collapsed and recycled
from some star in Plank Time, a nanosecond into the big burn,
atoms which now construct your heart, its unweary sea motion

that floats the brain outward in a speculative atmosphere,
surrounded by those very unastonished stars,
or held off by a dusk leaving its high water marks
across a lemon field thirty years ago—a little yellow
smoke lifting to where the wind arrives
unannounced, speaking to no one.
                          You asked for it,
and so return to rifling pockets in your houndstooth coat
for the scraps and sea-blue palimpsests. This is full-time,
taking notes, all the reasonable alternatives exhausted
long ago: shepherd, theoretical physicist, key grip,
architect for the blind, action-hero. Nothing new there.
So you figured you'd better mix it up, keep things moving,
bring out the birds again, the pomegranates opening
with their martyred light. Or perhaps something more
au courant—the insomnia of waterfalls, the algorithmic
rhapsodies of words alone, that relative cellular automata
of language dissolving like comets in their bright ices
and dust?
                   But they'll know it's you when the string section
swells offstage and clouds slip into view in black & white
gliding beneath the bare feet of some old saint, (a handful
of Bernini sunbeams thrown in for special metaphysical effect.)
The clouds of course were white, church bells rinsing out
the March sky, cut out of sea-colored construction paper,
the floating absences then held before your bleached
home-room wall.
                  And here pigeons are homing above
the sun-drunk roofs, wings brazed in unison, white
again as native fishing skiffs also tethered on a line
to the blue, as your boy's white heart kite-like over a field
of alyssum on the way home from school—grey sweatshirt
tied about your waist, sparrow in the guise of sparrows,
you're barely above the level of the fence posts as dust
settles down the west. You're fooling no one, and five
will get you ten you're humming some sappy bars
from "Moonglow" or "Theme from the Moulin Rouge,"

thinking you'll soon throw off awkwardness in favor
of romantic sophistication as easily as Jimmy Dean flips
a smoke into the street or runs a comb through his ducktail
before he blasts off in a hot rod Ford. Next party, you'll keep
the calypso beat, dip and glide like Harry Belafonte
as the 50s drift off like fog, like the little sleep and dream,
which, at best, they were. What else could you call it now?
Beginner's Luck, Cheap Grace, the Last Bus Home?

                                                                And what
about all that air back there thick with a varnished light?
No point in ignoring your life now and giving in to style.
And fame? That pink fin-job flop-top Cadillac and its chrome
roared down the highway to Boca Raton twenty years ago.
Eduardo Pérez-Verdia knew, and he told me in 1962—being
a Senior and therefore a man in the world—that the secret
to success, especially as far as singing and Elvis Presley
were concerned, was a sexy mumbling. And though the great
poet has said, *Air is Air*, what is that to you? Corazon!
Close the Cantina! Send the men in pinstripes home.
Get the movie stars out of the surf. Roll up your sleeves
and praise the first thing that moves up there—what more
is there finally to have at heart?

                                               Twenty years—you keep
shaking yourself, looking for the angel's bones, the latest
lexicon of light. You sift the bromides and debris for that
kid's lucky pocket piece, lost between the matinee and home
as he flipped it into the winter sky above the shops—misplaced
emblem of an unconscious belief in almost everything under the sun.
Oh, it was only silver and worth a buck, but it had a bird
whose wings—sometimes standing on a foothill stone—flew out
of his ribs into the evening sky. I'd open both clenched fists
and feathers would blow loose up into the chorused clouds.

                                                                 Nothing
close to this, of course, took place, but to put it in perspective,
I put in more than my fair share of time on top of boulders,
longing and imagination working over-time as I addressed
whatever was glowing in the live wires of my bones, pin balling

atom to atom to the west and back with no way out, no way to open
my hands and lift off even a little at ground level, but there
nonetheless.

It wasn't wisdom, for I'd regularly gone down
in flames in Spelling and in Math; and it was nothing close to grace
for I'd watched the girls, a sunflower haze all about them
as they spelled everything and walked away in the white music
of their blouses. But I could feel the voltage, those transactions
in the blood which kept me floating over the waxed linoleum
of a world where, despite low marks for comportment
and penmanship, I loved almost everything.

It strung me up
in the pear colored afternoons, in the pepper scented mists
of eucalyptus, and sang through me in a code sublime as the sea,
and I feared next to nothing alone along the jetty at low tide
or high in the avocado trees. Closing my eyes, my arms were full
of birds, and facing into the wind I named the nine planets
and nearest stars, called out five full Latin names for clouds.
I was a force in that murmuring world, a source, as it turned out,
unto myself. Yet I had nothing anyone was calling Promise—
for instance, I made no more of rain than the next one in line
as Monday poured down and the rooms went dim with breath.
Nor did I sport what could be called Confidence as I set off
on Saturdays in the neighborhood looking for friends with a hat
and six gun, a silver star on my shirt showing, if nothing else,
my allegiance to the skies.

Not long after this, the gentlemen
in bow ties and tweeds lectured me about "disinterestedness" and
"disassociation of sensibility"—something I was supposed to have
or my writing wasn't? I was reading Swinburne for the grand rhythm
of great angst and the emotional sea foam of the sound. I was told
to "absorb" Dryden, and thereby, at 19, improve my style in prose.
Bleeding Jesus, the paint came peeling off the walls,
and the clear voices of my age went unheard as I sat
in the campus grove closing my eyes between lines, coming back
to the world and wondering what I'd missed? A good bit of everything
was going in a blur. Who were the Manicheans exactly? Were we

or were we not in Cambodia, and what difference did it make
to the Vietnamese and the forests we'd already fried? What could I
possibly say about that when I was called on to stand and speak?
It wouldn't help then to engage in yet another Liberal Arts discussion
about what Aristotle considered to be truly "treeness"—
although I still loved trees, and like Matisse, always wanted
to keep the windows open to allow leaves and the calm labor
of their light to sift in. Looking up, I wondered if perhaps trees
weren't the last channels to heaven? Years later, drinking sherry
in an off-season flat, I'd stare through pines to the sea
or to the sea clouds and conclude that, Yes, that must be so—
loosely anchored to the earth as we were by the fourth glass
of fino, the hum and three-quarters glimmer of the soul
circling the amber bay off Barcelona.

                                      Perhaps I should give up
on trees, embellished by clouds or plain against the air,
palm fronds glinting with pewter as daylight glances down?
But I can't abandon the old loves for even two lines.
I'll admit I'll never make one comparison as surely
as they breathe light, and may well not live as long,
but against such odds as the dust builds up, I might as well
do the little that I can—home or half the world away
content myself with the cloud-sweep over umber hills,
yucca blooms carrying their immaculate prayers to the sun.
The short roots of my legs are trying to take hold—I shake
a little in the winds, the tides of orange blossom, sage, and salt—
I raise both hands to the light, surrender in my white shirt
to the inescapable sky, breathe out and say this.

Concerning Paradise

A little interrogation of the sky
and a thousand starlings break
from the trees—dark river of souls
working their way into the wind. And I
will never satisfy myself with the ambiguous
origins of clouds, above me all my life—
blank invoices which will one day
come due as we await revelation
of a sea-scrolled exegesis of light.

Who is there any more who doubts
our speck on the galaxy's bent rim will burn
out long before another breathing dot
on the pinwheel wonders where, for that moment,
in the stellar backwash, we ever were?
I haven't, by any means, finished with the earth,
though it seems I have no more ambition now
than the sparrows reasoning cheerfully
among the weeds.
                            Here, by the pittosporum,
by the plumeria, and bird of paradise's sun-brazed spikes,
by the jade plant jeweled with water drops,
it's clear that whatever is infinite will not be
approached by all the dull admonishments
of grief, thick as sea mist on the fan palms
along the cliff.
                            But there's no changing the course
of the blood as it confronts the moon—bright boat
without a country. Who would simply be
the apostle to evening's blue and cloud-shaped trees,
the insubordinate skies? I don't want to write
one more poignant poem about death, about the fissures
of a cosmos beyond my breath.

The empty road goes with me,
some last thing listening in the manzanita,
in the pause and distance of moonlight there
where the arroyo ends—space enough for St. Francis
to feed his heart again on the rocks,
for his calm colloquy to rise in hosannas
of atoms like the fragrance of sage
peppered across the night.
                    This will have to serve
as knowledge, suffice as prayer, one orbit
of somnambulant faith, one stop for the traveler
whose bones ache with the dead fires of creation,
whose soul—in its onion skin, its dust—
would just as soon drift toward that high snowy peak
beyond the thousand embers floating back up
from the lake.

            I'm still trying to do something here,
all this way from where I started. And though
the world is never going to be anything
more than the world—and the angels of dust
write our names across the backs of clouds—
I will not stop at nothing. So it matters
how the grass turns brown, how its yellow tips
burn, provisional as the stars.

About the Author

Christopher Buckley was raised in Santa Barbara, California, and educated at St. Mary's College, San Diego State University, and the University of California Irvine. He has spent many of his professional years teaching in California universities, and is now the the Chair of the Creative Writing Department at the University of California Riverside.

His most recent books of poetry include *A Short History of Light*, winner of the 1994 *Painted Hills Review* book award; and *Camino Cielo*, published by Orchises Press in 1997.

He has received a grant from the National Endowment for the Arts, a Fulbright Award in Creative Writing to Yugoslavia, four Pushcart Prizes, two Pennsylvania Council on the Arts Grants, and has twice received the Gertrude B. Claytor Memorial Award from the Poetry Society of America. Other awards include a John Atherton Fellowship in Poetry to the Bread Loaf Writers' Conference and an artist's residency at the Ucross Foundation.

His poetry has appeared in *The New Yorker, Antaeus, Gettysburg Review, Ploughshares, The Kenyon Review, New Letters, POETRY,* and many other journals. His work has appeared in many anthologies, most recently in *The Second Set* (Indiana University Press 1996), edited by Komunyakaa and Feinstein. He has been the editor of several anthologies, and serves as an Associate Editor for *Poetry International.* His essays, reviews, and interviews appear in many journals nationwide and several have been anthologised.

Fall from Grace is Buckley's ninth book of poetry.